SCHOLASTIC

25 Science Plays
for Beginning Readers

Sheryl Ann Crawford and Nancy I. Sanders

NEW YORK • TORONTO • LONDON • AUCKLAND • SYDNEY **Teaching**
MEXICO CITY • NEW DELHI • HONG KONG • BUENOS AIRES *Resources*

To my daddy, John M. Streib, who instilled in me a sense of nature's wonder and who took me back to the Indiana farm through his wonderful stories. —S.C.

To my sister, Laura Jackson, the most outstanding science teacher I know. Thanks for inspiring me with your love of animals, enjoyment of nature's beauty, and dedication to your students! —N.I.S.

Cover design by Maria Lilja; cover illustration by Jo Lynn Alcorn
Interior design by Sydney Wright; interior illustrations by Kate Flanagan

ISBN-13: 978-0-545-07268-7
ISBN-10: 0-545-07268-9
Copyright © 2000 by Sheryl Ann Crawford and Nancy I. Sanders
All rights reserved.
Printed in the U.S.A.

3 4 5 6 7 8 9 10   40   15 14 13 12

Contents

Introduction

Listening to the sounds of a thunderstorm, observing seeds sprout, or trying to count the twinkling stars in the night sky are doors to discovery and exploration for young children. Through the wonder of their five senses, children eagerly open their minds to learning about science in the world around them.

The plays and activities in this book tap this natural curiosity and will make science concepts come alive for your students while at the same time strengthening their reading skills. Each play contains vocabulary appropriate for beginning readers. In addition, many of the plays include rhyme, repetition, and predictable text. These features encourage student participation and repeated readings, a technique that helps students improve automaticity and fluency, a critical component of reading comprehension.

Using the Plays

Begin by reviewing vocabulary in a play that may be new to students. Then read the play aloud and model good reading behaviors by pointing out ways in which pacing, expression, punctuation, and inflection provide meaning clues.

Choral and echo reading are excellent approaches for fluency practice. Choral reading (in which the teacher and students read together as a group) encourages students to read at the same pace and with the same phrasing and intonation as the rest of the group. In echo reading, you read a line and students repeat it, echoing your expression, tone, and pacing.

When students are ready to read the plays on their own, you'll find that they are flexible to use. Some of the plays contain individual parts. Others have parts for the entire class. Feel free to divide your class into groups as small or large as you desire and have groups read each part aloud. Soon your students will be reading fluently as they learn about science in a lively and enjoyable way!

—Sheryl Ann Crawford and Nancy I. Sanders

What the Research Says
"Reading fluency refers to the ability of readers to read quickly, effortlessly, and efficiently with good, meaningful expression."

(from *The Fluent Reader* by T.V. Rasinski)

4

Curriculum Connections

Amazing Animals

The Spider Song

Spiderweb Math

Invite children to make spider headbands to wear when performing this play. Here's how:

☼ Measure a 2-inch-wide strip of construction paper to fit around the head.

☼ Glue eight 1- by 6-inch paper strips around the headband to form the spider's legs. Curl the leg strips with a pencil.

☼ Draw eight dots on the front of the headband for eyes.

For added fun when performing this play, go outdoors and use chalk to draw a giant spiderweb on the playground. Have children take positions at different points around the web.

Fly High, Butterfly!

Butterflies in Flight

Let students create butterflies to use when performing the play: Decorate round coffee filters with colored markers. Clip the filters onto spring-type clothespins to make butterflies. Paint empty bathroom tissue tubes green or brown to represent chrysalises. When dry, stuff the butterflies inside the chrysalises. As children perform the play, have them hold their chrysalises. At the point in the play when the butterfly emerges from the chrysalis, tell children to pull out theirs. At the end of the play, invite children to hold their butterflies high in the air and let them fly them around the room.

Hatching Ducks

We're Hatching!

Your whole class can perform this play using the following motions:

We are little baby ducks, awake inside our eggs.
(Crouch down on the floor in a little ball.)

Peck, peck, peckity-peck!
(Pretend to peck with your nose.)

We tap and poke out our legs.
(Stick out one leg, then the other.)

Crack, crack, crackity-crack!
(Pretend to peck again with your nose.)

Hooray! We're hatching today.
(Stretch out your arms.)

Quack, quack, quackity-quack!
We're ready to eat and play!
(Stand up, flap your wings, and walk around.)

There's No Place Like Home

What Is Your Home Like?

Have students sit underneath their desks. Then say, "Pretend that you are a rabbit inside your burrow. What is your home like?" List children's responses on chart paper. Repeat this process with new sheets of chart paper for animals such as fish, bees, or some of the animals depicted on page 22, and let children pretend to be those animals. Also encourage children to describe their own homes. Afterward, invite children to illustrate the charts. Then display them on a bulletin board and discuss how the homes are alike and different.

Home for Sale

Ecosystem of a Pond

For this play, design a backdrop that represents the ecosystem of a pond. Try to place it at children's eye level. Make the pond by covering the

background with a large rounded piece of blue craft paper. Create reeds by stapling twisted strips of brown and green craft paper along the sides of the pond. Have children use construction paper, colored cellophane, pipe cleaners, and other craft materials to make the animals described in the play as well as other animals that are found in a pond. Staple the pictures to the board.

When Nighttime Comes

Nocturnal Puppets

Here's a fun and easy way to make puppets for this play. To make a sleeping animal, glue eyelashes cut from black construction paper onto the folded bottom of a paper lunch bag. Under the fold, glue eyes cut from paper to make the animal look awake. Let students decorate the bags to resemble different nocturnal animals in the play (mice, skunks, owls, and so on). Invite children to make their animals look like they are awake while you read the play aloud. Afterward, describe different situations—the sun shining or the stars twinkling, for example—and tell children to make their puppets look like they're awake or asleep, according to whether it is night or day.

Winter Friends

Winter Graphing

Encourage children to bring in photos or magazine pictures of wild animals. (Or have old issues of nature magazines on hand.) On the bulletin board, make a "Winter Friends" graph with three columns labeled "Stays Awake," "Hibernates," and "Migrates." Help children mount their pictures on the graph in the appropriate columns, and discuss what each animal does during the winter months. Children may need help researching the behavior of some animals.

Once Upon a Food Chain

Make a Food Chain

Divide the class into groups of four or five. Cut 12- by 18-inch construction paper lengthwise into strips. Give one strip to each student. On the chalkboard, make a list of members of various food chains. Have each child choose one item from the board and draw it on the strip of paper. Then make food chains from the strips. For instance, one chain might consist of pictures of the sun, a flower, a moth, a frog, and a hawk. Staple each strip of paper into a circle that goes through the previous strip. Display the chains by hanging them from the ceiling.

All About Me

A Monster Meal

A Vote for Nutrition

Give each child two paper plates. Have children decorate one plate with a smiling face and the other with a frowning face. On the chalkboard, list different foods such as potato chips, candy, carrots, and apples. For each food, have children hold up the smiling face or the frowning face to indicate whether or not it's nutritious. Encourage children to share why they voted as they did. Have them suggest foods that make up a complete and nutritious meal.

Body Beat

Feel the Rhythm

Encourage children to clap their hands in a steady rhythm as they read the play aloud. Afterward, play a game of "Simon Says" that encourages identification of the different parts of the body. For example, say, "Simon says point to your heart" or "wiggle your finger bones." If you don't say "Simon says . . . ," children who do the motion sit down. The last player still standing wins.

Too Smart for Germs!

Sharing Germs

Give children a visual demonstration of how germs are spread. Dip both sides of a damp sponge into a pan of flour. Have children stand in a line and pass the sponge down the line. Count to see how many children get flour on their hands. Discuss what might have happened if the sponge had had germs on it rather than flour. Explain that if someone had sneezed on the sponge, tiny germs would get on the sponge. Every child who then touched the sponge would get germs on his or her hands, just as they got the flour on their hands. Explain that germs also get on doorknobs, desks, pencils, and other things. Ask children to share why it is important to wash their hands before they eat and after they use the bathroom and to stay home when they are sick.

Something Tells Me

"Five Senses" Venn Diagrams

Take your students on a "Five Senses Walk" around your school neighborhood or through a nearby park. Provide a snack for them to eat along the way. During the walk, stop and ask students to identify the different ways they are using their senses. Afterward, use yarn or string to make a two-ring Venn diagram on the floor. (The rings should overlap and be large enough for students to sit inside.) Use tagboard strips to label one ring "Hearing" and the other "Sight." Ask children to sit inside the appropriate circle, according to the sense they relied on to perceive their favorite experience. (Some children may sit inside the intersection of the circles or outside the circles.) Ask children sitting inside the rings to describe their favorite experience on the walk. Then have the remaining children describe theirs. Next, make a three-ring Venn diagram. Label one ring "Taste," one "Touch," and one "Smell," and repeat the process.

Clean and Healthy Kids!

Teddy Bear, Teddy Bear, Wash Your Hands

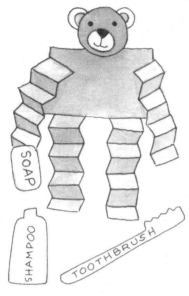

Help each student make a teddy bear from construction paper. For each bear's body, use a 9- by 12-inch sheet of brown construction paper. Cut another two sheets in half lengthwise for the arms and legs. Cut a 4-inch circle of brown paper for the head. Accordion-fold the legs and arms. Glue the arms, legs, and head to the body as shown. Draw the bear's face, and glue on 1-inch brown semicircles for ears. Cut construction paper to make a bar of soap, a toothbrush, and a shampoo bottle. Label each. Have children hold their bears as the class recites verses in unison—for example, "Teddy Bear, Teddy Bear, wash your hands" and "Teddy Bear, Teddy Bear, brush your teeth." Children place the soap, shampoo, or toothbrush in their bear's hand and pretend to have the teddy bear perform the appropriate action.

Plants and Seeds

Farmer, Farmer

Our Sunflower Garden

For each child, cut two sheets of 12- by 18-inch yellow construction paper in half lengthwise. Stack these four sheets on top of each other and staple across the top. Then show children how to create the different stages of a sunflower's growth on each page.

1. On the first page, draw the ground and then plant a sunflower seed by gluing it onto the paper.
2. On the second page, again draw the ground and glue on another sunflower seed. Then draw a little green shoot poking out of the ground.
3. Repeat steps 1 and 2 on the third page, but this time draw a taller green shoot with leaves.
4. On the fourth page, draw a full-grown sunflower. On the flower's face, glue several sunflower seeds.

Mount children's books on a bulletin board in a row so that all the first pages show. Label the board "Our Sunflower Garden." During the week, add a paper sun and rain cloud to the board. Turn the pages of the books every few days, tacking them to the board so that the next stage of the sunflower's growth shows.

At Home in a Tree

Build a Tree

Grow a large tree right in your classroom. Twist long strips of brown craft paper to make the trunk and branches. Staple these to a bulletin board so that the trunk hangs to the floor. Some branches may reach out over the ceiling. Add construction paper leaves to the branches. Children can use construction paper to make different animals that live in a tree. Tape or staple these to the branches. When the tree is finished, have children find out three facts about their animal, write them on an index card, and staple the card next to their animal.

That Time of Year

My Favorite Tree

Take a nature walk with children to look at different kinds of trees, or show them pictures or photos in magazines or field guides. Identify trees as deciduous or conifer. Encourage children to describe each tree's characteristics (shape, type of leaves, seeds, and so on). Then invite them to draw a picture of their favorite tree. On a bulletin board, make a graph with two columns. Label one column "Deciduous" and the other "Conifer." Help students mount their pictures in the appropriate columns on the graph.

A Seed Surprise

A Guessing Game

Bring in a variety of fruits that have seeds, such as apples, oranges, pinecones, green peppers, and avocados. Cut each fruit open and let children observe the different kinds of seeds. Then give each child half of a file folder. (In advance, cut a 1-inch hole from the center front of each folder.) Let each child choose a different kind of seed. Have children glue their seeds to the front of their folders and write "*Child's name*'s Seed." On the inside, have them draw a picture of what their seeds will become. At the bottom of the picture, have them write "Surprise!" Then let children swap folders, examine the seeds, and peek through the hole to guess what each seed will become. Then they can open the folders to see if they guessed correctly.

It's Harvest Time!

Harvest Math

Bring in a pumpkin, an apple, and an ear of dried Indian corn for each group to examine. Divide the class into groups, and challenge each group to estimate the measurements of each and record their guesses. (Have them estimate circumference, length, width, height, weight, number of seeds, and so on.) Afterward, help children find the actual measurements of each fruit and record their results. How do each group's estimates compare with the actual measurements?

Earth and Sky

Let's Go Exploring!

Let's Explore Some More!

Divide the class into small groups. Have each group choose one environment or ecosystem to research, such as a rain forest, swamp, or river. (Encourage children to select environments that differ from those used in the play.) After groups have found several facts about their topic, together rework the play to incorporate the new facts. (Rhyme isn't necessary.) Then read aloud the new version of the play.

All Aboard the Earth Train!

A Train Ride

To perform this play, create a train by arranging two rows of chairs for children to sit on as they read. Seat the remaining children on the floor next to the train. You will be the conductor. Pretend to ride to different habitats, such as mountains, deserts, and the ocean. Ask the passengers on the train to describe the types of animals they might see as they visit each area. The rest of the class can then act out each animal that the passengers see. Finish by returning to school on the train. After the play is finished, choose new volunteers to ride the train.

My Shadow, My Friend

Shadow Guessing

Use an overhead projector to play this game. Lay a small object on the glass and project its silhouette on the wall. Have children take turns guessing what the object is. Use objects that make surprising shadows (a round soup can turned sideways makes a rectangular shape, for instance) as well as objects that don't create a shadow, such as a clear piece of plastic. After children try to guess each object, discuss the similarities and differences between each object and its shadow. Note how shadows show the outline of an object but not its features.

Alphabet Clouds

Cloud Pictures

On a day when there are clouds in the sky, go outdoors and have children observe the clouds and describe any pictures they see. Back inside, give students cotton balls and glue to make cloud pictures on a sheet of blue construction paper. When dry, hang these pictures flat on the ceiling or clip them to a clothesline strung across your classroom. Invite children to lie on their backs and look up at the cloud pictures. Encourage them to share their thoughts about the pictures they made.

Four in a Storm

Listen to a Storm

As children read this play aloud, invite them to create the sounds of a passing storm. For the wind, have them rub the palms of their hands together in a back-and-forth motion. For the sound of raindrops, let them drum their fingertips lightly on a hard surface such as a desktop. For a heavy rainstorm, have them rapidly pat their thighs with their hands. They can create thunder by stamping their feet. To make the storm sound like it's going away, have them repeat the motions in the opposite order. Afterward, ask children in what ways the different noises they made sounded like those of an actual storm.

Big Dipper

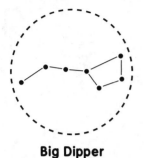

Cassiopeia

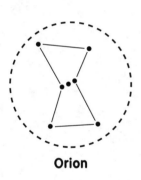

Orion

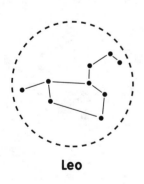

Leo

Twinkle, Twinkle, Pretty Stars

Peek at the Stars

Invite students to decorate the outside of large, empty cardboard oatmeal containers by covering them with decorated construction paper. Then have them trace the bottom of the containers onto black construction paper and cut out the circles. (These circles may need to be trimmed slightly to fit inside the containers.) Let children use silver star stickers to make a constellation pattern on their black circles. They can copy actual constellations (see left) or design their own. Then have them glue the black circles inside the bottom of the oatmeal container so the constellations can be seen when children peek inside. Let children spend time peeking inside the containers to view one another's constellations.

Some Like It Hot, Some Like It Cold

Our Solar System

Divide your class into ten groups and assign one planet or the sun to each group. Ask each group to find information about the appearance of that planet (or the sun). Help children locate pictures in library books or on the Internet. (Check out www.seds.org/nineplanets/nineplanets/nineplanets.html.) Then give each group a large sheet of construction paper and crayons to draw a picture of their planet or the sun. Have children cut out their celestial bodies and then mount them, in correct order, on a strip of dark blue bulletin board paper that spans a classroom wall. Let each group label their planet (or the sun) and share several facts about it.

The Spider Song

(to the tune of "London Bridge")

Characters

Big Spiders   Little Spiders

Big Spiders: See how fast we spin our webs,

Little Spiders: Spin our webs,

Big Spiders: Spin our webs.

Little Spiders: Round and round we spin our webs,

All: They grow bigger!

..................➤

Big Spiders: See the bugs stick to our webs,

Little Spiders: To our webs,

Big Spiders: To our webs.

Little Spiders: Strong and sticky spiderwebs

All: Catch our breakfast!

Big Spiders: Webs are strong in rain and wind,

Little Spiders: Rain and wind,

Big Spiders: Rain and wind.

Little Spiders: Webs are homes that we live in.

All: We are spiders!

The End

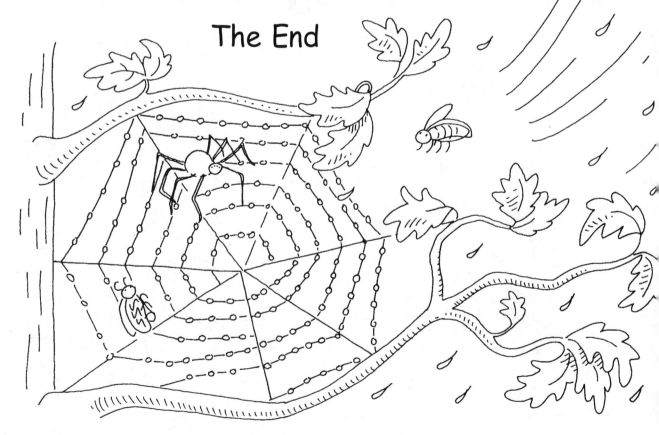

Fly High, Butterfly!

Characters
Children 1–12

Child 1:   This is the tree …

All: where the fuzzy wuzzy caterpillar lived.

Child 2:   This is the branch
that grows on the tree …

All: where the fuzzy wuzzy caterpillar lived.

Child 3:   These are the leaves it ate
that grow on the branch …

Child 4:   that grows on the tree …

All: where the fuzzy wuzzy caterpillar lived.

Child 5:   This is the chrysalis it built
after eating the leaves …

Child 6:   that grow on the branch
that grows on the tree …

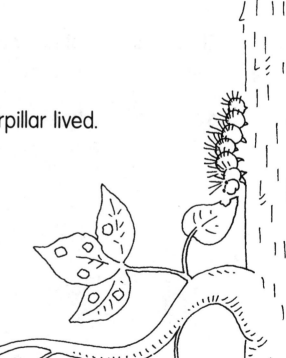

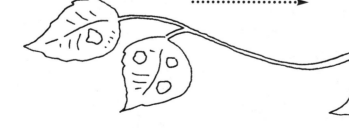

All: where the fuzzy wuzzy caterpillar lived.

Child 7:   This is the butterfly
that pushed out of the chrysalis …

Child 8:   that the caterpillar built
after eating the leaves …

Child 9:   that grow on the branch
that grows on the tree …

All: where the fuzzy wuzzy caterpillar lived.

Child 10:   This is the sky where the butterfly flies
after pushing out of the chrysalis …

Child 11:   that the caterpillar built
after eating the leaves …

Child 12:   that grow on the branch
that grows on the tree …

All: where the fuzzy wuzzy caterpillar lived.
Good-bye, butterfly! Fly high!

The End

Hatching Ducks

Characters

Ducks 1–3

Duck 1:   We are little baby ducks,
        awake inside our eggs.

Duck 2:   Peck, peck, peckity-peck!
        We tap and poke out our legs.

Duck 3:   Crack, crack, crackity-crack!
        Hooray! We're hatching today.

All: Quack, quack, quackity-quack!
        We're ready to eat and play!

The End

There's No Place Like Home

Bees 1–3:   There's no place like home!

Bee 1:   It's inside an old tree,

Bee 2:   Where the queen lays her eggs.

Bee 3:   There's sweet honey to eat.

Bees 1–3:   Do you know what our home is called?

All: A hive!

Bears 1–3:   There's no place like home!

Bear 1:   It's a deep, dark cave

Bear 2:   With piles of warm leaves.

Bear 3:   It's a nice place to sleep.

Bears 1–3:   Do you know what our home is called?

All: A den!

Ants: 1-3:   There's no place like home!

Ant 1:   It's a small hill of dirt

Ant 2:   With paths dug inside

Ant 3:   And rooms for our eggs.

Ants 1-3:   Do you know what our home is called?

All: An anthill!

Beavers 1-3:   There's no place like home!

Beaver 1:   It's made from sticks and mud.

Beaver 2:   Our door is underwater.

Beaver 3:   It sits near a dam.

Beavers 1-3:   Do you know what our home is called?

All: A lodge!

·····················➤

Birds 1–3:   There's no place like home!

Bird 1:   It sits high in a tree,

Bird 2:   A round bed of sticks and grass.

Bird 3:   Our eggs stay warm and safe.

Birds 1–3:   Do you know what our home is called?

All: A nest!

Bears and Beavers: Homes can be big or small.
Homes can be high or low.

Birds, Bees, and Ants: Our homes may be different.
But one thing is just the same.

All: There's no place like home!

The End

25 Science Plays for Beginning Readers   Scholastic Teaching Resources

Home for Sale

Characters

Salesperson Toad	Mom Turtle
Dad Turtle	Little Turtle

Turtle Family: We'd like to buy a new home.
It has to be just right for turtles.

Salesperson Toad: Have I got the home for you!
If you love pond life,
you'll love this home!

Turtle Family: Show us!

Salesperson Toad: There are all kinds of plants here,
like moss and reeds and water lilies.

Dad Turtle: Plants for food and plants to hide in.

Mom Turtle: Small plants for animals to eat.

Little Turtle: Tall plants for me
to play hide-and-seek in!

Salesperson Toad: There's plenty of water, too.

Dad Turtle: Water for animals to swim in.

Mom Turtle: Water for animals to drink.

Little Turtle: Water for me to play, slip, and slide in.

Salesperson Toad: If you want a busy pond, this is it!

Dad Turtle: A busy pond is a healthy pond.

Mom Turtle: Everything we need to live is here.

Little Turtle: Wait! Not everything!
I need some new friends.

Salesperson Toad: I've been saving the best for last.
Look!

Little Turtle: Wow! I see new friends!
Dragonflies and turtles,
toads and tadpoles!

Dad Turtle: We'll take it!

Mom Turtle: Home, sweet home!

Salesperson Toad: Sold!

The End

When Nighttime Comes

Characters

Mice	Skunks	Night Crawlers	Coyotes	Owls
Crickets	Lightning Bugs	Anteaters	Bats	Moths

Mice: When nighttime comes, mice start their day. It's time to tiptoe, eat, and play.

Crickets: When nighttime comes, while others sleep, crickets like to chirp and cheep.

Skunks: When nighttime comes, skunks hunt quite well. But if we're scared, we'll really smell!

Lightning Bugs: When nighttime comes, we shine so bright. Each lightning bug has its own night-light.

Night Crawlers: When nighttime comes, out creep the worms, from underground to wiggle and squirm.

Anteaters: When nighttime comes, we use our long noses.
No ants are safe where the anteater goes.

Coyotes: When nighttime comes, we hunt and prowl.
When it's dark, coyotes like to howl.

Bats: When nighttime comes, we make screechy calls.
Bats fly and hunt and don't hit walls.

Owls: When nighttime comes, owls' big eyes
watch for dinner running by.

Moths: When nighttime comes, moths fly about.
If we fly inside, please let us out.

All: When nighttime comes, some must sleep.
But we stay up and don't count sheep!

The End

Winter Friends

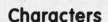

Characters

Phone	Deer	Bear
Groundhog	Snake	Blue Jay

Phone: Ring! Ring! Ring!

Groundhog: Hello?

Deer: Hi, Groundhog! It's snowing today.
Do you want to come outside and play?

Groundhog: Not today.
I'm digging down deep.
It's time to close my eyes and sleep.

Phone: Ring! Ring! Ring!

Snake: Hello?

Deer: Hi, Snake! There's ice on the lake.
Will you come out to play hide-and-seek?

Snake: Not today.
I can't play at all.
I'm going to sleep in a tight little ball.

Phone: Ring! Ring! Ring!

Bear: Hello?

Deer: Hi, Bear! It hasn't stopped snowing.
The snowballs are soft
and just right for throwing.

Bear: Not today.
I'm warm in my den.
When spring arrives,
I'll come out again.

Phone: Ring! Ring! Ring!

Deer: Hello?

Blue Jay: Hi, Deer! Winter is here.
Come out and play tag
with the birds and the other deer.

Deer: Sure! I'm glad I can play
with my winter friends.
The others are sleeping
until cold weather ends.

The End

Once Upon a Food Chain

Characters

Storyteller 1	Sun	Cow	Farmer
Storyteller 2	Grass	Baby	

Storyteller 1: Once upon a food chain, there was the sun.

Sun: I am the sun!
I am bright and yellow and warm.
I help make plants grow and grow!

Storyteller 2: Once upon a food chain,
there was some green grass.
The sun made it grow and grow.

Grass: I am the green grass
growing thick and tall.

Storyteller 1: Once upon a food chain,
there was a hungry cow.

Cow: MOO! I'm a hungry cow!
I want green grass!

Storyteller 2: The cow ate the green grass.
It ate and ate.
The grass helped the cow
make rich, white milk.

⋯⋯⋯⋯⋯⟶

Storyteller 1: Once upon a food chain,
a farmer held her child.

Baby: WA-A-A-A! I'm hungry! WA-A-A-A!

Farmer: I am the farmer! My child needs milk!

Storyteller 2: The farmer milked the cow
and gave the milk to her child.
The milk helped the child grow and grow.

Storyteller 1: All this talk about the food chain
is making me hungry!
I wish we had a snack.

Storyteller 2: Look! I have a bag of peanuts.

Storyteller 1: Once upon a food chain,
the sun made these peanuts grow and grow.

Storyteller 2: Once upon a food chain,
two hungry storytellers
ate them all up!

Both Storytellers: The End!

A Monster Meal

Characters

Monster Mom   Little Monster 1
                Little Monster 2

Monster Mom: Little Monsters, clean off your plates.
Eat your tin cans.

Little Monster 1: But Mom, we don't like tin cans.
They break our teeth.

Little Monster 2: May we have fruit instead?

Monster Mom: Fruit? Good little monsters
never eat fruit!
Why would you want fruit?

Little Monster 1: We like fruit. It's tasty,
and it's fun to count the seeds.

Little Monster 2: Apples and oranges
are good for you!

Both Little Monsters: We want to be strong
and healthy monsters!

Monster Mom: Apples and oranges sound terrible.
                     But okay, you can have fruit.
                     First, eat your shoes.

Little Monster 1:   But Mom, we don't like shoes.
                          They're too hard to chew.

Little Monster 2:   May we have vegetables instead?

Monster Mom: Vegetables? Good little monsters
                     never eat vegetables!
                     Why would you want vegetables?

Little Monster 1:   We like vegetables.
                          They have bright colors,
                          like green, yellow, and orange.

Little Monster 2:   Carrot sticks and green beans
                          are good for you!

Both Little Monsters: We want to be strong
                              and healthy monsters!

Monster Mom: Vegetables sound terrible.
                     But okay, you can have vegetables.
                     Just make sure to eat
                     your plates when you're done!

 The End

25 Science Plays for Beginning Readers   Scholastic Teaching Resources

Body Beat

Characters

Chorus 1   Chorus 2

Chorus 1:   Bones. Bones. We have plenty of those.
What do bones do? Does anyone know?

Chorus 2:   We have bones. Bones are good!
They help us stand tall like we should!

Chorus 1:   Muscles. Muscles. Do we have a few?
What kinds of things do muscles do?

Chorus 2:   We've got muscles. We've got some.
They help us walk, jump, and run!

Chorus 1:   Skin. Skin. Who has skin?
It's the covering that we live in.

Chorus 2:   From head to toe, we're wearing skin.
Nothing falls out! Germs can't come in!

Chorus 1:   Lungs. Lungs. Air in. Air out.
What are lungs all about?

Chorus 2:   Lungs help us breathe the air we need.
Just take a breath and see what we mean!

Chorus 1:   The heart. The heart.
Where's that part?
Does everyone here have a heart?

Chorus 2:   Yes! Hearts pump blood
from our head to our feet.
Thump! Thump! Thump! Thump!
Do you hear the beat?

Chorus 1:   The brain. The brain.
Did you hear what I said?
Do we all have a brain
in our heads?

Chorus 2:   Our brains are big.
They know a lot.
We think and learn.
Brains never stop!

All: We feel healthy! We feel good!
Just the way a body should!
Bones and muscles.
Skin and lungs.
Our heart. Our brain.
This was fun!

The End

25 Science Plays for Beginning Readers   Scholastic Teaching Resources

Too Smart for Germs!

Characters
Child 1   Child 2   Germs

Child 1:   Look, I have carrot sticks for us to share.

Child 2:   Thanks!

Child 1:   Oops! I dropped them in the dirt!
I'll wipe off the dirt.
Then we can eat them.

Germs: Oh, boy! They'll never know we're here!

Child 2:   Look out!

Child 1:   Look out for what?

Child 2:   You're about to eat germs for lunch!
Germs can make you sick!

Germs: Shhh! Don't tell! We're hiding!

·····················➤

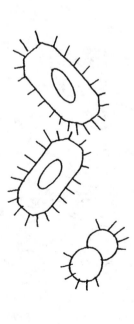

Child 1:   I don't see any germs.

Child 2:   Of course not!
Germs are too small to see.
But we know they're there!

Child 1:   You can't trick us, germs!
We know you're there!

Germs: Uh-oh. These kids are smart.

Child 2:   Let's wash off those germs with water.
Let's wash our hands, too.

Child 1:   Good idea! Did you hear that, germs?
You're going down the drain!

Germs: Oh, boy! We love the drain!
Just think of all the other germs we'll meet!

Child 2:   So long, germs!
Now you can't stick to our carrot sticks!

**Both
Children:**   We're too smart for germs!

The End

Something Tells Me

Characters

Children 1–3

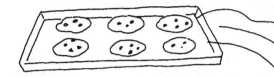

Child 1:   Something tells me there are colors in a rainbow.

Child 2:   Something tells me there are pictures in a book.

Child 3:   Something tells me my friends are playing outside.

All: That something is our eyes!
We're using our sense of sight.

Child 1:   Something tells me cookies are baking.

Child 2:   Something tells me it's time to take out the trash!

Child 3:   Something tells me there's a candle burning.

All: That something is our noses!
We're using our sense of smell.

Child 1: Something tells me this kitten is soft.

Child 2: Something tells me this rock is hard.

Child 3: Something tells me this worm is slimy!

All: That something is our fingers.
We're using our sense of touch!

Child 1: Something tells me a bird is singing.

Child 2: Something tells me a horn is honking.

Child 3: Something tells me my friend is whispering.

All: That something is our ears!
We're using our sense of hearing.

Child 1: Something tells me this lemon is sour.

Child 2: Something tells me this juice is sweet.

Child 3: Something tells me this popcorn is salty.

All: That something is our tongues.
We're using our sense of taste.

All: We see, we smell, we touch,
we hear, we taste.
Something tells us
having five senses is great!

The End

25 Science Plays for Beginning Readers   Scholastic Teaching Resources

Clean and Healthy Kids!

Characters	
Group 1	Group 2

Group 1:   Yuck, yuck, yuck!
             We get dirty every day.

Group 2:   But, but, but…
             we don't have to stay that way!

All: At home, at school, or at play,
             we keep clean and healthy every day.

Group 1:   Splash, splash, splash!
             We wash our hands with soap.

Group 2:   Brush, brush, brush!
             We brush our teeth like this.

All: At home, at school, or at play,
we keep clean and healthy every day.

Group 1: Wash, wash, wash!
We wash our hair like this.

Group 2: Scrub-a-dub-dub!
We scrub our body in the tub.

All: At home, at school, or at play,
we keep clean and healthy every day!

The End

Farmer, Farmer

(to the tune of "Teddy Bear, Teddy Bear, Turn Around")

Characters

Corn Plants Groups 1–7

Corn Plants Group 1: Farmer, farmer, dig, dig, dig.

Corn Plants Group 2: Farmer, farmer, drop the seeds in.

Corn Plants Group 3: Farmer, farmer, pat the dirt down.

Corn Plants Group 4: Farmer, farmer, water the ground.

Corn Plants Group 5: Farmer, farmer, feel the hot sun.

Corn Plants Group 6: Farmer, farmer, it warms the ground.

Corn Plants Group 7: Farmer, farmer, the plants are out!

All: Farmer, farmer, jump and shout!

The End

At Home in a Tree

Characters

Teacher Owl	Caterpillar	Cow
Robin	Squirrel	

Teacher Owl: At school today, we will talk about trees.
Who knows what trees are good for?

Robin: Trees are great for birds to build nests in.

Teacher Owl: Yes. Trees are good for robins.
Okay, school is over. It's time to go home.

Caterpillar: Wait! Trees are good for more than that!
Trees are great for insects to live in, too.
And their leaves are tasty treats to eat!

Teacher Owl: Yes. Trees are good for robins and insects.
Okay, school is over. It's time to go home.

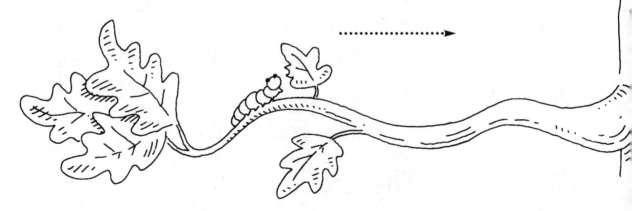

25 Science Plays for Beginning Readers   Scholastic Teaching Resources

Squirrel: Wait! Trees are good for more than that!
Trees are great for storing our food.

Teacher Owl: Yes. Trees are good for robins, insects, and squirrels.
Okay, school is over. It's time to go home.

Cow: Wait! Trees are good for more than that!
On hot summer days, trees are good to sit under.
Trees help cows stay cool!

Teacher Owl: Yes. Trees are good for robins,
insects, squirrels, and cows.
Okay, school is over. It's time to go home.

Robin: Teacher Owl, where is your home?

Teacher Owl: Oh! I forgot!
Trees are a great place for owls, too!
We sit high in the branches and look for food.
Okay, school is over. It's time for all of you
to come and see my great tree home!

The End

That Time of Year

Maple Tree: Feel the wind? It's fall!

Oak Tree: It's that time of year again!

Aspen Tree: Time for our leaves
to fall to the ground.

Birch Tree: And cover it
with lots of bright leaves.

All Deciduous Trees: Let's go!

Tree Chorus: Red, yellow,
orange, and brown.
See the leaves
float to the ground!

Pine Tree: Feel the wind? It's fall!

Cedar Tree: It's that time of year again!

Fir Tree: Time to watch our friends drop their leaves.

Spruce Tree: But we'll stay green and hold on to ours.

All Conifer Trees: Don't our colors look great together?

Tree Chorus: Some trees stay green all year round.
                              Some trees have leaves that fall to the ground.
                              Trees make this a beautiful place
                              and give the earth a nice bright face!

The End

A Seed Surprise

City Friend: I found a little black seed today.
I wonder what it will become.

Country Friend: Plant it and find out.

City Friend: Okay. I'll leave it on the ground
and wait for it to grow.

Country Friend: You need to dig a little hole,
then drop the seed in
and cover it with dirt.

City Friend: Okay. I think it will grow
into a little black raisin
because it's a little black seed.

Country Friend: Wait and see.
You will be surprised.

City Friend: I don't know what to feed my little seed.
How about some soda pop?

Country Friend: Seeds need just soil, water,
light, and air to grow.

..............➤

City Friend: That's easy! I'll water my seed.
Will it grow into a little black raisin?

Country Friend: Wait and see.
You will be surprised.

City Friend: Look! My seed is starting to grow.
A green vine is growing.

Country Friend: It's growing and growing,
just like it should.

City Friend: Look! It's not a little black raisin.
It grew into a big watermelon!
How did it do that?

Country Friend: Inside each seed is a baby plant.
After the seed is planted, it starts to grow.

City Friend: Do big plants like trees
start from a little seed?

Country Friend: Yes, even the tallest ones.

City Friend: A little seed can be a big surprise!

The End

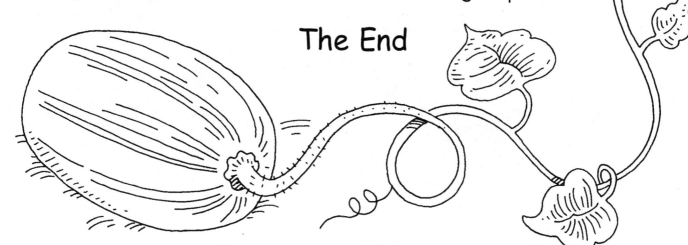

It's Harvest Time!

Characters

Wampanoag (WAHM-puh-NOH-ahg) Indian
Pilgrim

Wampanoag: Look! The pumpkins are big and round. It's harvest time!

Pilgrim: Let's have a harvest party and eat pumpkin pie!

Wampanoag: We'll save some pumpkin seeds. We'll plant the seeds and grow pumpkin vines.

Pilgrim: That sounds good to me.

Wampanoag: Look! The apples are red. It's harvest time!

Pilgrim: Let's have a harvest party and eat apple pie.

25 Science Plays for Beginning Readers Scholastic Teaching Resources

Wampanoag: We'll save some apple seeds.
We'll plant the seeds and grow apple trees.

Pilgrim: That sounds good to me.

Wampanoag: Look! The corn is tall and ripe.
It's harvest time!

Pilgrim: Let's have a harvest party!

Wampanoag: We'll save some seeds from the corn.
We'll plant the seeds and grow more corn.

Pilgrim: Let's eat corn pie!

Wampanoag: Corn pie? That's silly.
We don't make corn into a pie.
We just eat it like it is.

Pilgrim: I know. I was just being "corny."
Let's have a harvest party
and eat our good food!

Both: It's harvest time!

The End

Let's Go Exploring!

All: Come on! Let's go exploring.
Around the earth we'll roam.
So many places to see
before we head for home.

Explorer 1: Let's sail across the ocean.

Explorer 2: We'll ride upon the waves.

Explorer 3: Let's watch for whales and jellyfish

Explorer 4: and dolphins as they play!

Explorer 5: Let's explore the sandy shore.

Explorer 6: We'll wander far and wide.

Explorer 7: Let's look for shells and starfish

Explorer 8: and crabs that like to hide.

Explorer 9: Let's go inside a dark cave.

Explorer 10: We'll shine flashlights all around,

Explorer 1: on secret lakes and wet rock walls,

Explorer 2: where bats sleep upside-down.

Explorer 3: Let's walk along a forest path.

Explorer 4: There's so much to see and hear:

Explorer 5: Tall trees, foxes, chattering squirrels,

Explorer 6: singing birds, and quiet deer.

Explorer 7: Let's travel through the desert.

Explorer 8: I wonder what we'll see there.

Explorer 9: Bright sun, cacti, lizards, snakes,

Explorer 10: and white sand everywhere!

All: Let's look for Earth's great riches.
We'll listen for its sounds.
Come on! Let's go exploring!
Let's go the whole world round!

The End

All Aboard the Earth Train!

Characters

Conductor   Passengers 1–12
Train

Conductor: All aboard the Earth Train!
Bring your cameras.
You'll see some great things!

Train: Choo-choo-choo-choo! Toot! Toot!

Conductor: First stop on Earth is a rain forest!

Passenger 1:   I'm getting off to take pictures
of bright red frogs!

Passenger 2:   Me too! I will take pictures of tall, tall trees.

Passenger 3:   Me too! I will take pictures of plants
that grow on other plants.

Train: Choo-choo-choo-choo! Toot! Toot!

Conductor: Next stop on Earth is the desert!

Passenger 4:   I'm getting off to take pictures
of that sharp cactus.

Passenger 5:   Me too! I will take pictures of lizards
running through the sand.

Passenger 6:   Me too! I will take pictures of desert foxes.

Train: Choo-choo-choo-choo! Toot! Toot!

Conductor: Next stop on Earth is the wetlands!

Passenger 7:   I'm getting off to take pictures of trees
covered with moss.

Passenger 8:   Me too! I will take pictures of birds
floating on the water.

Passenger 9:   Me too! I will take pictures
of swimming crocodiles.

Train: Choo-choo-choo-choo! Toot! Toot!

Conductor: Next stop on Earth is the Arctic!
                        Put on your heavy coats. Br-r-r-r!

Passenger 10:   I'm getting off to take pictures of seals playing.

Passenger 11:   Me too! I will take pictures of big, big icebergs.

Passenger 12:   Me too! I will take pictures of polar bears
                        chasing our train!

Conductor: Polar bears chasing our train?
                        Hurry! Everyone back on the train!

Train: Choo-choo-choo-choo! Toot! Toot!

Conductor: Next stop, the train station.
                        Everyone off!

All Passengers: Let's go again!
                        There are lots more things to see on our Earth!

Conductor: All aboard the Earth Train!

Train: Choo-choo-choo-choo! Toot! Toot!

The End

My Shadow, My Friend

(to the tune of B-I-N-G-O)

Characters: Chorus 1   Chorus 2

All: I have a friend that comes and goes.
                   And Shadow is its name, oh!

Chorus 1:   Shine a light on me.
                   Then my friend you'll see!

All: My friend looks like me,
                   And Shadow is its name, oh!

Chorus 2:   I see my shadow on the wall.
                   It always does what I do.

Chorus 1:   Jump and spin around!
                   Bend down, touch the ground!

All: Look! It's on the ground!
                   And Shadow is its name, oh!

Chorus 2:   When it's dark, I look around.
                   I cannot see my shadow.

Chorus 1:   Shine a light on me.
                   Then my friend you'll see!

All: My friend looks like me,
                   And Shadow is its name, oh!

The End

Alphabet Clouds

Characters

Chorus   Children A to Z

(Each child may take two parts.)

Chorus: Water drops rise up in the air very high.
                        They join with dust to make clouds in the sky.

All Children: Each cloud's color, size, and shape
                        tells us what weather is on its way.

Chorus: We see fun shapes in the clouds that move.
                        What do different clouds look like to you?

A and B: I see a cloud that looks like an ape.
                        I see a buffalo taking shape.

C and D: I see a cowboy wearing one shoe.
                        I see a donkey cooking a stew.

E and F: I see an elf reading a map.
                        I see a frog taking a nap.

G and H: I see a goose popping some corn.
                        I see a horse blowing a horn.

25 Science Plays for Beginning Readers   Scholastic Teaching Resources

I and J: I see an insect wearing a tie.
              I see a jellyfish floating by.

K and L: I see a kitten baking some bread.
              I see a lion riding a sled.

M and N: I see a moose blowing its nose.
              I see a nurse smelling a rose.

O and P: I see an octopus waving, hi!
              I see a peacock eating a pie.

Q and R: I see a queen running in a race.
              I see a rocket zooming in space.

S and T: I see a spider wearing eight socks.
              I see a tiger climbing big rocks.

U and V: I see an umpire calling, "You're out!"
              I see a vet caring for a trout.

W and X: I see a walrus on the phone.
              I see an x-ray of a bone.

Y and Z: I see a yucca plant in the sun.
              I see a zebra chewing gum.

All: We see fun shapes in the clouds that move.
              What do different clouds look like to you?

The End

Four in a Storm

Characters	
Wind 1–4	Lightning 1–4
Rain 1–4	Thunder 1–4

Wind 1:   Whoosh! Shoosh!

Wind 2:   Trees move and bend!

Wind 3:   Hold on to your hat!

Wind 4:   It might fly off with the wind!

Wind 1–4:   I am the wind, your whispering friend.

Rain 1:   Plink! Plink! Plop!

Rain 2:   Drizzle! Drip! Drop!

Rain 3:   Pull on your boots!

Rain 4:   Put on your raincoat!

Rain 1–4:   I am the rain. Drip! Drip! Drop!

25 Science Plays for Beginning Readers   Scholastic Teaching Resources

Lightning 1:	CRRR-RACK! FLASH!
Lightning 2:	Streams of light.
Lightning 3:	Look at the show!
Lightning 4:	But don't fly your kite!
Lightning 1–4:	I am lightning, fast and bright!
Thunder 1:	RUMBLE, RUMBLE.
Thunder 2:	CRASH AND BOOM!
Thunder 3:	Cover your ears.
Thunder 4:	Hear me shake the room.
Thunder 1–4:	I am thunder. RUMBLE! CRASH! BOOM!
All:	Rain and thunder, lightning and wind. What a LOUD and BRIGHT storm we've been!

The End

Twinkle, Twinkle, Pretty Stars

(to the tune of "Twinkle, Twinkle, Little Star")

Characters	
Group 1	Scientist
Group 2	

Group 1:   Twinkle, twinkle, pretty stars,
Can you tell us what they are?

Scientist: Stars are gases burning bright,
Blazing fire that gives us light.

Group 2:   Twinkle, twinkle, stars of light,
Burning gases make them bright!

Group 1:   Twinkle, twinkle, near and far,
Which one is the closest star?

Scientist: Our closest star is called the sun,
Shining light on everyone.

Group 2:   Twinkle, twinkle, see the sun,
The closest star to everyone.

················>

Group 1: Twinkle, twinkle, stars of light,
Why do stars just shine at night?

Scientist: Bright light from the sun each day
hides the starlight from far away.

Group 2: Twinkle, twinkle, sun so bright,
shines all day, but not at night.

Group 1: Twinkle, twinkle, one, two, three,
Can you count the stars for me?

Scientist: There are trillions, big and small.
We can never count them all!

Group 2: Twinkle, twinkle, one, two, three,
Trillions shining! Look and see!

Group 1: Twinkle, twinkle, stars up high,
Far beyond the deep blue sky.

Group 2: Stars that look like shining dots
are blazing gases burning hot.

All Children: Twinkle, twinkle, pretty stars,
Now we know just what they are.

The End

Some Like It Hot, Some Like It Cold

Characters	
Koala	Polar Bear

Koala: Let's take a trip and find a new planet to live on.

Polar Bear: We'll zoom through space.

Koala: I wonder which planet it will be.

Polar Bear: Just remember, I like it cold!

Koala: But I like it hot!

Polar Bear: Let's go to Pluto.

Koala: Pluto is a dwarf planet.

Polar Bear: Pluto is the farthest from the Sun.

Koala: It's too cold on Pluto.

25 Science Plays for Beginning Readers Scholastic Teaching Resources

Polar Bear: I like it cold.

Koala: But I like it hot!

Polar Bear: Okay. Let's go to Neptune and Uranus.

Koala: Neptune looks like a blue star.

Polar Bear: Uranus is made of a lot of gas.

Koala: It's too cold on Neptune and Uranus.

Polar Bear: I like it cold.

Koala: But I like it hot!

Polar Bear: Okay. Let's go to Saturn.

Koala: Saturn has pretty rings around it.

Polar Bear: It's cold on Saturn. I like it cold.

Koala: But I like it hot!
I know, let's go to Jupiter!

Polar Bear: Jupiter is the biggest planet.

Koala: It's hot on Jupiter. I like it hot.

Polar Bear: But I like it cold!
I know! Let's go to Mars.

Koala: Mars is half as big as Earth.

Polar Bear: Mars looks red and orange.

Koala: It's too cold on Mars.

Polar Bear: I like it cold.

Koala: But I like it hot!
Let's go to Mercury and Venus.

Polar Bear: Mercury is the planet closest to the Sun.

Koala: Venus is covered with clouds.

Polar Bear: It's too hot on Mercury and Venus.

Koala: I like it hot.

Polar Bear: But I like it cold!

Koala: Hey! We don't need to take a trip through space.

Polar Bear: Earth is the best planet for us to live on!

Koala: Earth has cold snow for you
and warm sun for me.

Polar Bear: It has air to breathe and water to drink.

Both: Earth has living things—like us!
Living anywhere else would be unBEARable!

The End

25 Science Plays for Beginning Readers   Scholastic Teaching Resources